UPROOTING

LEAVING THE ABUSE CYCLE

UPROOTING

LEAVING THE ABUSE CYCLE

EDITED BY

JADE ROSINA MCCUTCHEON

KRISTIN THOMAS

A Publication of The Poetry Box®

©2023 The Poetry Box®
All rights reserved.
Poems, Stories, Text, and Artwork copyright by individual authors and artists.

Copy Editing, Line Editing, & Book Design by Shawn Aveningo Sanders
Cover Design by Shawn Aveningo Sanders
Cover Artwork: "Silenced" by RMae, also on page 17

No part of this book may be republished without permission from the publisher, except in the case of brief quotations embodied in critical essays, epigraphs, reviews and articles, or publisher/author's marketing collateral.

ISBN: 978-1-956285-41-3
Library of Congress Control Number: 2023910139

Published in the United States of America
Wholesale Distribution by Ingram Group

Published by The Poetry Box®, September 2023
Portland, Oregon
Website: ThePoetryBox.com
Email: Shawn@ThePoetryBox.com

Please Note:

*In some of the survivor stories and accounts,
a letter is used in place of a name to protect the woman involved.*

Table of Contents

Introduction — 11

Section One

Autobiography in Five Short Chapters (Portia Nelson) — 15

Chapter I — 17
- Art: Silenced (RMae) — 17
- Statistics & The Power of Silence — 18
- Survivor Account: *I was sixteen and in love…* — 19
- Art: She Somehow Makes It through Each Day (Jarmac) — 19
- Poem: Matryoshka (Dale Champlin) — 20
- The Ten Years War (Shannon Rose Riley) — 21
- Photo: Torn by the Shore (Jade Rosina McCutcheon) — 23
- Poem: This Charming Man (Dale Champlin) — 24
- Poem: Facedown (Sherri Levine) — 25
- Accepting the Reality of Abuse (Jade Rosina McCutcheon) — 26
- Poem: Hatred (Jade Rosina McCutcheon) — 27
- Art: Meeting Artemis (Frances Greenwood) — 28
- Poem: Meeting Artemis (Frances Greenwood) — 28
- Poem: In Public (K. Thomas) — 29
- Photo: I See You (Jade Rosina McCutcheon) — 30
- Poem: Unprocessed Trauma (Candice Campo) — 30
- Poem: Those Who Stand and Watch (anonymous) — 31
- Survivor Account: *R was only five years old…* — 32
- Art: Fracture (Frances Guerin) — 32
- Poem: Fracture (Frances Guerin) — 33

Poem: Hairline Break (Candice Campo)	34
Art: Heartbeat ((Jade Rosina McCutcheon)	34
Poem: Unseen (Rmae)	35

Chapter II — 37

Art: I Fall in Again (Dakota Reddekopp)	37
Poem: Play House (Candice Campo)	38
Poem: Less (K. Thomas)	38
Poem: That Night (Dale Champlin)	39
Poem: Pain (Jayme Sue)	40
Poem: To You, My Sister (Marilyn Johnston)	41
Poem: Sisterhood (Jade Rosina McCutcheon)	42
Art: Sisterhood (Ann Altman)	42

Chapter III — 43

Art: Alive (Rebecca Smith)	43
Poem: What He Doesn't Know (Diana Blackstone-Helt)	44
Photo: Anger Traps the Angry (Jade Rosina McCutcheon)	45
Poem: Echoes of Captivity (Ann L. Lovejoy)	46
If You Fall into the Hole Again	47
Poem: A Kind of Disaster (Sherri Levine)	48
Poem: A Heart Wildly Pounding (Kelley Morehouse)	49
Poem: The Silent Voice (Jade Rosina McCutcheon)	50
Poem: To a Broken Child (LDM)	51
Poem: Exposed (Susan Woods Morse)	52

Chapter IV — 53

Art: Eyes Over Cloud (Rmae)	53
Poem: Free from Monsters (K. Commander)	54
The Drama Triangle	56

Paradox (Cassandra Summer) ... 57
Poem: Measuring Up (Candice Campo) ... 58
Poem: Recovery (Rmae) ... 59

Chapter V ... 61
Art: You Are Not Alone (Rebecca Smith) ... 61
Poem: Spirit (Jade Rosina McCutcheon) ... 62
Poem: Single (Summer Harlan) ... 62
Triggers and Healing (Cassandra Summer) ... 63
Poem: Hindsight (Summer Harlan) ... 64
Art: Be Kind—Not Nice (Rebecca Smith) ... 65
Poem: Roots (Jade Rosina McCutcheon) ... 66
Photo: Sentinel (Jade Rosina McCutcheon) ... 67
Poem: New Growth (Cassandra Summer) ... 68

SECTION TWO

Healthy Relationship Behaviors & Dynamics ... 71
Art: I Will Protect You (Jarmac) ... 71
The Good Mother Exercise ... 72
Early Childhood Trauma ... 72
The Good Mother & The Wounded Child ... 73

Trauma Impacts & Resilience ... 75
Parts of the Brain ... 75
Fight, Flight, or Freeze ... 75
How Trauma Affect Survivors ... 76

Power & Control ... 81
Survivor Account: *L was married at seventeen…* ... 81
The Power and Control Wheel ... 82

What Is Gaslighting?	85
Art: I Don't Know Who I Am Anymore (Jarmac)	86
Examples of Gaslighting	87
Navigating the Legal System	89
Survivor Account: *After calling her sister…*	89
Advice from Oregon Attorney, David Johnson	89
Survivor Account: *J was granted temporary restraining order*	90
Filing a Restraining Order	90
Uprooting	91
Poem: There Will Be Days (Shawn Aveningo Sanders)	92
Photo: Flowering (Jade Rosina McCutcheon)	94
Resources for Finding Help	95
National	95
In Oregon	96
Acknowledgments	105
About the Contributors	107

Introduction

This collection of poetry, art, and writing by survivors of domestic and sexual abuse is a work of love by all involved. The abuse of women continues because of the power of silence. The more women speak out, the more attention this issue receives. As editors, we chose to divide the first section of the book into five chapters, each based on a stanza from Portia Nelson's (1920-2001) popular poem "Autobiography in Five Short Chapters." Each chapter is a stage of the cycle of "uprooting" and breaking free from cycles of abuse. Yes, we might *fall into* that *hole in the sidewalk* three times, but on the fourth time we *walk around it*. And the fifth time, we *choose another street*.

The contributing writers, poets, and artists of this book range from award-winning to those who have never been published. We are deeply thankful to each contributor for speaking out. Our deepest gratitude to Shawn Aveningo Sanders at The Poetry Box press for giving this work the opportunity to be picked up by survivors worldwide. We also give thanks to Sable House, all the amazing women who work there and those who use Sable House as a resource. A big thank you to Judy Breuer from the Domestic Abuse Intervention Program for her assistance with using the Power and Control Wheel.

It is our intention that this book is useful to all who read it, whether it is just a reminder that you are not alone, to find helpful resources in the back of the book, or to inspire you to begin your own artistic journey as a survivor.

If you appreciate this anthology and feel you can give a small donation, Sable House would gladly welcome your contribution as they continue to be a resourceful haven for women and their children. Please make your check payable to Sable House and mail to P.O. Box 783, Dallas, OR 97338. You can also donate on-line at sablehouse.org/donate.

—Jade Rosina McCutcheon & Kristin Thomas
co-editors

SECTION ONE

Autobiography in Five Short Chapters
Portia Nelson

Chapter I
I walk down the street.
There is a deep hole in the sidewalk.
I fall in.
I am lost … I am helpless.
It isn't my fault.
It takes forever to find a way out.

Chapter II
I walk down the same street.
There is a deep hole in the sidewalk.
I pretend I don't see it.
I fall in again.
I can't believe I am in the same place.
But, it isn't my fault.
It still takes a long time to get out.

Chapter III
I walk down the same street.
There is a deep hole in the sidewalk.
I see it is there.
I still fall in … it's a habit … but,
my eyes are open.
I know where I am.
It is my fault.
I get out immediately.

Chapter IV
I walk down the same street.
There is a deep hole in the sidewalk.
I walk around it.

Chapter V
I walk down another street.

Chapter 1

I walk down the street.
There is a deep hole in the sidewalk.
I fall in.
I am lost ... I am helpless.
It isn't my fault.
It takes forever to find a way out.

—Portia Nelson

Silenced by RMae

Statistics & The Power of Silence

More than half of Oregon's female population—that's 1 million women and girls—have been sexually assaulted. More than a third of Oregon women have faced domestic violence.

- In 2019, sexual violence impacted over 40% of American women over their lifetimes.
- 298,628 women were sexually assaulted or raped in 2020.
- Only 310 out of every 1,000 sexual assaults are reported to law enforcement.
- There are over 463,000 rape victims in America each and every year.
- 90% of adult rape victims are women.

According to the Department of Health and Human Services, there are over 60 million survivors of childhood sexual abuse in America—approximately 20% of the population.

> "Victims of abuse are usually stressed and confused about their situation. This confusion can block their confidence to report the issue, or they ignore it, thinking it will go away in time. It doesn't.
>
> "Often the channel to address the issue leads to the legal department, but law firms can be a breeding ground for bully protection. Those with money or positions of power often have greater access to lawyers. They can quickly exhaust the victim's ability to afford legal support, and they know it. The power abusers are often in a position to control the legal outcomes.
>
> "As a result, these cases often go unreported, undetected, and unchallenged, because the victim feels that the threat of action could be worse than the original form of abuse. This creates a vicious cycle in which the perpetrators feel that getting away with the crime empowers them to continue their abusive behavior."
>
> —Petrina Coventry

Abuse is about power and control, and it can grow over time as one person becomes more determined to maintain what they think is control over the situation.

That person can be a mother, father, sister, brother, wife, husband, boyfriend, girlfriend, or work colleague.

Survivor Account

I was sixteen and in love, I didn't know anything except that I wanted to be with this person for the rest of my life....

P was raised in a violent household; she and her sisters and brothers were silenced by their father's beatings and their mother's fear. As the eldest, she took a lot of the heat, including the ugly desires of her father. No one seemed to notice or care—not at the schools, the church, or in the neighborhood—they all looked right through her. The first person who paid any attention to P was F who went to the same school. He started to suggest they meet after school. Sometimes he would have a flask with some alcohol, other times weed. P liked the attention. F wasn't like her father; he was kind and funny and listened to her. F had it rough too, and they bonded over their shared abusive childhoods. By seventeen, P had left school, was pregnant, and living with F who was going from job to job. By twenty-five, P was a battered and broken woman, unable to leave F, and the victim of domestic violence.

She Somehow Makes It Through Each Day ~Jarmac

MATRYOSHKA

Dale Champlin

She is
a little used-to-be-
girl more like a woman
now or a capsized boat
beached on her life's
rocky shore
washed
up. Sticky
with resentment.
Before this impasse
she tried to sell the world
one contradiction at a time.
It only broke her spirit
so she shredded herself
into ribbons, hid behind
veils of addiction,
encased herself in
armor of relapse
and recovery, her
wall-clock ticks
like a metronome
each second repeated.
She could care less if she
is so over her shithole life
screaming her banshee screams
that only cockroaches could hear.
Their quick dive for cover her razor-
sharp voice howling like a dirty wind
blown up the valley of her skirt sleeves
rivers chanting story after hair-raising
story sleeping instead of dying her head
buzzes and her restless ribcage constricts
watery notes burbling indistinguishable
as her thoughts disappearing like stars in
daylight. She has such small shoes to fill.

The Ten Years War

Shannon Rose Riley

Once upon a time, there was a little girl who swore revenge against her father. She was just five years old.

What caused his anger that night, she wasn't sure, but she knew her father had been very drunk—the kind of drunk that made his eyes appear deeper in his skull, wet with the color of blood, the kind of drunk that turned him into a raging monster.

It must have been around her bedtime because she was pretending to sleep on the little cot in the corner of her parent's bedroom. Her mom and dad were also in the room, standing by their bed, silhouetted by the lights on the nightstands.

"You're lying. You're a liar."

"I'm not lying, John! I swear!"

"Why were you there? Why were you talking to him?"

"I didn't…"

Her words were swallowed up by the vicious blow that landed across her face. Blood sprayed from her mouth.

She tried to leave the room but he was hot on her heels. As she ran down the hallway towards the front door, he swung at her from behind. Following behind him was the little girl, screaming at the top of her lungs.

"Daddy, please, stop it!"

"Where are you going? Are you trying to run to him?"

"John, please! Please stop!"

LaVaughn had opened the front door and he lunged forward to grab the top of her beehive hairdo. He pushed forward, tackling her to the ground outside the apartment door. She screamed at the top of her lungs as his full body weight fell upon her. He scrambled up quickly in spite of being so drunk and proceeded to drag her down the stairs to the front of the building by her hair.

"John, please!"

"Daddy, stop it!"

By now, neighbors furtively poked heads outside of cracked doors, closing them again just as quickly. Someone yelled down from the second floor,

"Keep it quiet!"

But no one did anything to help her, except the little girl. She didn't run away, she didn't leave her mom's side, and she kept yelling at her dad to stop. Suddenly he did stop—the girl saw a strange look of surprise on his face as if he'd just arrived in the hallway and wasn't sure what was going on. Perhaps he was afraid someone had called the cops, perhaps his daughter's cries had snapped him out of it. All the little girl knew was that the punching and pulling of hair had stopped. She looked at her mom, whose face was tear-stained and bloodied. Her lips, swollen and cracked. Her green eyes, puffy and dark. Her beehive completely undone, clumps of red hair on the carpet in the hallway.

His rage had subsided just enough for the little girl to get her mom back into the apartment. She walked her to the bedroom and told her that it would be OK but as soon as the words were out of her mouth, he was running back in behind them, worked up again. And once again, John began to hit LaVaughn in the face and head with the very fists that had won him a Golden Gloves boxing prize at age 16.

The little girl had had enough and began to hit and kick this man, her father. She didn't care anymore if she was supposed to show respect, if she was supposed to love him. She punched him as hard as she could with both hands—using the fists that he himself had taught her to make and he turned around suddenly. He looked down at the tiny girl and her small fists pummeling him… and he laughed. He laughed at her and spun her around by one arm, spanked her on the ass, and told her to get into her bed. His laughter was sickening—it was as if he was proud to see his daughter punching him, using her fists, as if he were happy to send her back to bed, happy in his power.

As she lay on her little cot in the corner of the room, she felt the sting of that laughter and the powerless shame of being sent to bed. She watched him through her fingers as he continued to hit her mother—she heard the sobs, she heard the begging—and she promised herself right then and there that she would get even one day, and that she would save her mom.

It would take 10 years to make good on that promise. I am that little girl.

Torn by the Shore ~Jade Rosina McCutcheon

This Charming Man
Dale Champlin

Every gesture he makes is full of music,
he's so handsome and rich.
He says *let's go to a party*—
but won't take you home when you want—
or—*let's take a walk down by the shore*
and he holds your hand too tightly
except you're embarrassed and don't want him
to get the wrong impression so you go along,
the entire coastline stuck in your throat
you don't trust him completely
afraid he might knock you down
and he does—suddenly you hear
your ankle rip—the ligaments torn
by his weight crashing down full force
and you don't grimace or cry out
telling yourself this time will soon be over
and time does jump forward
he lets you out of his car
where you limp to your door. But your ankle
will never be the same.

FACEDOWN

Sherri Levine

He untucks his shirt
pulls down his zipper
pushes my head on his lap.
To me, it looked like the neon pink
monster sea worm
I once saw in a magazine.
Penis worm, they called it,
undulating at the bottom of the sea,
its dimple-eyed body pulsated
like my mother's twisted blue veins.
What would it be like to float on the surface,
facedown, without sinking?
Arms loose and long,
would I hear the sound
of my heart beating?
Now, with my head still pressed
down by his football hands,
I'm swimming laps
at the Y,
stretching one arm, then the next,
each breath no different
than the one
that carries me
to the other side.

ACCEPTING THE REALITY OF ABUSE

Jade Rosina McCutcheon

As children we often don't know why an adult man, often one we should trust, is doing this to us and we block it out in order to survive. For some women I have worked with over the years, the habit of "not being present" is embedded in their nature. This is a short story about M who was repeatedly raped by her father and his friends from the age of three to ten. "I would see myself up on the ceiling, looking down on him as he did this to me. I couldn't feel what he did anymore, I would just use my mind to not be there." What M was doing could be called "getting out of body" or leaving the present reality for an imaginary one where she wasn't being hurt.

By the time I was working with her, she was fifteen, in a shelter, and had been in lock up situations for several years. We would talk about how she escaped as a child and how she then used alcohol and drugs as a teen to do the same. Getting "out of it" was the habit she had learned in order to survive unspeakable things being done to her. As a child she was the only one who could save herself, as her mother was also always "out of it." Jumping out of body is a common behavior for survivors of sexual assault, especially as children.

We have no language as young children, we have no rights, we are solely dependent on the adults who brought us into this world.

Hatred

Jade Rosina McCutcheon

It is in the body, the shudder,
frozen breath
iced in arrested limbs,
red panic, kicking pale
all because
you knocked on my door.

I knew then your rage
against me
overwhelmed
the world.

MEETING ARTEMIS

Frances Greenwood

She rose on the horizon
like the moon on a hot night
a massive red ball, out of shape.

Her profile formed by the slopes of the mountains speaks,
"scream the truth, summon your tiger"
as I stand upon the crumbling cliff
she says the cat is out of the bag
no bishop's crook or papal bull
can conceal his lies
or sins forgiven in the dark box
banal hypocrisy illumines the public eye.

So rise like mythic Persephone and Europa
and face the west wind
that blew you into womanhood.

In Public
K. Thomas

He is always in control.
He doesn't lose control of his temper,
Or lose control of his emotions.

Because if he lost control,
Or lost his temper
He would have beat your ass standing in the Walmart checkout line
When the grocery bill was $2 higher than he allowed
But he waited until you were alone

He would have shoved and slapped you at the family BBQ calling you a whore
When you hugged your favorite uncle
But he waited until you were alone

He would have kicked you in the stomach in the hospital exam room
When the chlamydia he gave you, was his proof of you cheating
But he waited until you were alone

He would have grabbed you by the hair and call you a stupid cunt in front of his
Coworkers when the sandwich you made him didn't include fucking pepper jack cheese
But he waited until you were alone.

I See You ~Jade Rosina McCutcheon

UNPROCESSED TRAUMA

Candice Campo

She knew it would not be too long before she felt it again, the heavy feeling.
A dirty, soaked washcloth, balled up in the corner.
Spreading mold in the shower stall of her soul.

THOSE WHO STAND AND WATCH

anonymous

And you,
you just stood there
in the same home
silent while he beat us
beat us
raped us.

Mother you,
were still,
were not there,
absent in heart,
head, soul.

How could you
witness the beating down of your own children?
How could you
allow the destruction of their self-worth?

You left us
at the mercy of a pedophile
a cruel, hard man
and never   ever   tried
to protect
us.

What would you call yourself?

I remove the name "mother"
from you

you are
"betrayer."

Survivor Account

R was only five years old when her uncle started to come into her room at night. Her mother had an alcohol problem and her mother's boyfriends also visited R at night. This continued until she was fifteen, taking away every precious part of her, little by little, until she was so far away from herself, she had no center. Her self-esteem was almost non-existent—her voice was silenced for a long time.

Fracture ~Frances Greenwood

Fracture

Frances Greenwood

In a grove of trees in Galway
a white crane stands on the riverbank
watching water run over smooth stones

the trees say, trust us
as a clock with legs runs by
and a striped figure emerges from a pit
full of rage and repetitions.

A frenzied nun in black robes beats a child with a cane
screaming: *God sees everything*
you will burn in hell forever
unless you confess to the priest.
Children immobilized in plaster casts,
dragged into the dark confessional
where a priest shears off limbs
with a chainsaw, a strange smile on his face

Bless you my child, I absolve you.

A blue-eyed woman clothed in gold
runs by with a clock.

I am leaning against the bark of the tree.

Hairline Break

Candice Campo

Sometimes, I can feel it.
The weight.
The tangled entrenchment of confusion swirled within longing,
planted and tended to by my subconscious.
An innate growth that peaks out from underneath the fragile surface
when a hairline break occurs.

Heartbeat ~Jade Rosina McCutcheon

Unseen

RMae

Intimidation was the monster that always gripped
tha green-handled cake knife.
Control was the motive that split my face open,
a fight for life.
Jealous rage was the beast that squeezed
my throat that night.
Manipulation through twisted wrists and crushed feet,
unseen pain without a light.
Love bombing, gaslighting, fake grief,
that's got my stomach not feeling right.
Too many denial-turned heads, shame throwing & guilt
only add to our survival fight.

Let's open minds & hearts
to slow that madness of another's plight.
Because the battles we are all fighting
might NOT be seen through eyesight.

CHAPTER II

I walk down the same street.
There is a deep hole in the sidewalk.
I pretend I don't see it.
I fall in again.
I can't believe I am in the same place.
But, it isn't my fault.
It still takes a long time to get out.

—Portia Nelson

I Fall in Again ~Dakota Reddekopp

PLAY HOUSE

Candice Campo

You know not what I've been through
Play with your doll house he once said
And then his hands would linger and he'd pull me into bed
Almost near my birthday, just after turning four
I got the pointed finger, and heard the words that knifed out
Whore.

LESS

K. Thomas

His hands slide across my ass
It wakes me up
From my foolish sleep

In my cotton armor
I convince myself I'm safe
Lying in sweaty slumber

His hands slide between my legs
My body naked to his touch
My armor pushed away

I drift away in my mind
Keeping time to a broken
Rhythm of bed springs

His body slides off mine
And I am still
Less than I was before

THAT NIGHT
Dale Champlin

There is nothing to be afraid of,
he told the little girl,
I'm your brother after all,
your reflection in the mirror,
your bookend. Come and sit
on my quilt and I will tell you
a bedtime story. Listen
to the rain on the roof,
how the wind thrashes
the leaves. I will put
my hands into your nightie
to keep you warm. Put your face
near mine so I can smell your breath.
Put your feet between my thighs
and don't call for mother, she doesn't
want to hear you snivel. Come under
the covers with me and lift up
your nightgown just so. I will rock
you to the patter of acorns
hitting the roof. Don't worry—
it's just an owl hooting
in the tree outside the window.

That screeching you hear
is only a branch
needling the windowpane.

Pain

Jayme Sue

Violent noises crashing in my mind
the walls that bind my brain
cage the memories
silent, no words escape
feelings too intense
encased in a body too fragile to hold them.

Tremors wrack my physical body
as my mind explodes
trauma, pain, endless cycle
of healing and wounds reopening.
Can I shut off this terror that follows me
causes me to obsess over these things.

I cannot unhear the things I've heard
I cannot unsee the things I've seen
from the demon of elusive imagery
existing only inside,
where it hides and eats away at sanity.

Peace forsaken as this war pits me against myself
forget about expressing this to the world
forget caring about bringing it to the light
how long do I decide
how long do I hide
I've need of a saving grace.

Nowhere to go inside the cage of my mind
I've felt so much pain ripping away at parts of me
lost feeling alone
desiring more than what I've had before
future, what does it have in store.
Forever waiting, wanting more
I've lost too much
can I recover these parts lost
or are they gone, existing no more.

To You, My Sister

Marilyn Johnston

Like a head bowed
at the foot of a cold shrine,
you could see inside the grave
of an unknown god—
eyes trapped in sulking anger,
like dried-up pools
after a summer
of no rain.

You were so alive once.
As girls we'd played and laughed
until our mothers threatened
to separate us—
before you became
the puppet they carved of you.
Someone else behind your song,
your voice far away.

It's late, but everything
after that came next—
the crystal meth road you drove,
the soulless men you trusted,
the swallowed lies.
Your dreams, swept up like hard pebbles,
first were strewn, then formed boulders
between us, cutting off the path.

We once pledged,
"Let's be the same wound
if we must bleed,"
but then your cuts
opened deep
and could not heal.
They left you raw.
Gone.

Sisterhood

Jade Rosina McCutcheon

I lie down
inside emerald green
shrugging off the dust of separation
a soft fluttering
as the habit of just "me"
        once disconnected
        from the garden of my sisters
falls away
let's connect
see what
magic patterns we can weave
working together.

Sisterhood ~Ann Altman

Chapter III

I walk down the same street.
There is a deep hole in the sidewalk.
I see it is there.
I still fall in … it's a habit … but,
my eyes are open.
I know where I am.
It is my fault.
I get out immediately.

—Portia Nelson

Alive ~Rebecca Smith

What He Doesn't Know
Diana Blackstone-Helt

This angry shove is familiar to her.
So is this pain echoing along her spine
As she tumbles into the bathtub.
It's a lot like the pain
She tried to forgive and forget
When her back slammed against the bedroom door
Some weeks ago…
The last time he promised *never again.*

The same enraged eyes glare at her.
The same mocking voice hurls its venom.
But suddenly
Somehow
This time is different.
In the mirror behind him
She gazes into the tired eyes
Of a woman who looks like her
But is not her.
It's someone else.
And she knows for the first time
That woman can be free.

What he doesn't know—
What he can't possibly know
Is what happens when she's no longer afraid—
When her fear turns to contempt.
At that moment
Each shove
Each slap
Each punch
Only feeds her power
Until she's ready
To fly away.

Then he will assault the air
And it will recoil—
BAM! Right between the eyes.
His angry words will become
Bitter vines
Imprisoning him in a poison green cell
Of his own making.
And she'll know she can't rescue him
Even if she wanted to.

Anger Traps the Angry ~Jade Rosina McCutcheon

ECHOES OF CAPTIVITY

Ann L Lovejoy

. . . the exhibit areas explore the themes of capture, living conditions, news and communications, those who wait, privation, morale and relationships, and escape and freedom.
  —National Prisoner of War Museum exhibit, Andersonville, GA.

Capture

She went willing to him believing
in his "I love you I want you I need you"
written from a country far away.

Capture is easy in unknown places –
smudged from dust and sun, her
contour maps don't show terrain.

And no one is there to help her. Even
the language fails her – words don't work
to stop the next part, traveling through the dark.

Journey

Every day she commutes an hour of freedom
tightly timed not to trigger jealousy. Not
like a prisoner of war who journeys once.

Torture

Yelling in the night, smashed against walls.
His agents say his words – "you bruise easily
why ever won't you take your vitamin K?"

Coping

In the rocking chair quiet, nothing moves
maybe a tiny breath goes in and out
to keep brain working, joy to think.

Release

Freedom hurts. Only glaciers move this slow
and calve off in great shuddering chunks
swamping the sea, drowning a thousand days.

We are programmed from our childhood experiences to accept abuse as "normal" when we are in a relationship. Without consciously realizing it, we fall in love and fall into a dark hole where the abusive scenario we grew up with plays itself out.

If you fall into the hole again and notice that you are back in the same cycle of abuse, realize that:

- It takes time
- Notice the cycle
- Forgive yourself – you were programmed to accept abuse
- Talk to your wounded child
- Make a safety plan with a counsellor, welfare worker, shelter worker, advocate
- Give yourself time to find a safe way out
- Don't rely on the opinions of friends or family
- You do not deserve disrespect
- You do not have to live with cruelty
- You are the one who will save you

A Kind of Disaster
Sherri Levine

I've known earthquakes in my home
pots being thrown, plates crashing into
one another, drapes closing
in the afternoon.
I've felt the boom! boom!
above my bed
and watched my dolls shake
their heads.
I don't know what it must have felt like
afterwards,
what she must have felt.
I never got to see her
exhausted
mess
on
the floor.
Still
I lay there waiting
for something to happen,
or change—
for her to come and get me
so I could hold her.

A Heart Wildly Pounding

Kelley Morehouse

The feeling came to me, waking this morning,
of my childhood years. Not in technical terms nor literal,
but a sense of slipping through a parent's hand in mid-air,
an accident, like a fragile egg about to hit the floor.

The moment where the heart is pounding. Not like an egg,
either, because I never hit the floor. But, like being high
up in the sky and dropped from a jet plane, followed
by the long descent down, the fall spanning a lifetime,
falling and falling, flailing and possibly dying at first
in the very cold atmosphere until I revive
on the long tumble down. There is nothing, nothing
and nobody, but mouthfuls of empty air for years
of perpetual falling, all behind the scenes I invented
to survive. I cannot find the ground,
until the ground finds me.

It's a parent holding on, until they no longer do.
As far as I see in my blood-line, each child is dropped,
as much as no one ever planned to do so. My mother
and father dropped their descendants, as they themselves
were dropped. In turn, my siblings drop descendants,
and I am no exception. None of us see ourselves
in the downward plight—numb
to our heart wildly pounding.

THE SILENT VOICE

Jade Rosina McCutcheon

Grandmother Lil was beaten to pulp by Grandfather Bob
Baby Pat watched and when he grew older
he beat his wife Lulu while grandmother Lil watched
and his son Abel watched
and no-one cared.

Lulu went to court to get a little help
for Pat was breaking her bones.
The judge believed that families should stay together
sent her back to live with Pat.
Abel grew up and beat his wife
and so it goes.

To a Broken Child
LDM

Child, you are a part of a great flood of tears.

You suffer, but not alone;
Humanity suffers with you. Your pain is our pain.
Thousands of years have passed, gathering our tears
Into a great rolling swell which cannot be stopped.
It carries us along in its embrace.

When will it be enough?
Enough to break the dam and free each soul—
Enough to overflow the obstacles that trap us—

When?   Not yet.   Be patient, child.

Cry your tears with us, and we will welcome them.
We know your tears, for they are ours.
Comfort yourself, child, in our embrace.

Exposed

Susan Woods Morse

Black crows wheel and scream along with red-tail hawks overhead,
      early November mornings—the fish fulfilling their inescapable destiny,

and I remember a poem I once read. In it, a girl writes of gang rape
      and visualizes dying salmon, Pacific salmon with delicate insides exposed.

Years ago, at the Mokelumne River we watched them scatter useless seed
      in their final frenzy, trying to fling themselves up and over the fish ladders

thrashing
      pink
           bloated
                  with grayed lips and underbellies

their silence and the water's silence
      sharply punctuated by the thrust
           of the excited onlookers' cawing,
                ready to pounce on any remains,
                     the salmon ascending and dying all at once.

I think that is what she meant.

CHAPTER IV

I walk down the same street.
There is a deep hole in the sidewalk.
I walk around it.

—Portia Nelson

Eyes Over Cloud ~RMae

Free from Monsters

K. Commander

You were supposed to be safe.
You were supposed to love me,
but not like that.
Never like that.
You killed me.
A piece of me. Every time
you touched me.
In the backyard.
In your room.
In my room.
I was never safe from you. No escape.
You killed a piece of me. You took
my childhood.
You were the monster,
in the closet,
under the bed.
The evil in the dark.
Except,
You were real.
I couldn't escape you.
They said monsters weren't real,
But you were much, much worse.
So, I hid.
I hid under the covers. For years.
Years.
Afraid.
Terrified,
to attract attention
to myself
from you,
from monsters like you.
Because if you could do that…
That means they all will…
That means they're all predators…

Don't attract attention.
Stay quiet.
Be ugly.
They hunt the weak.
But.. I'm not weak.
This isn't my fault. I didn't ask for this.
You did this.
You did this to me.
I'm not weak.
You are.
I was a child. You knew better.
I've been living in fear,
I've been letting you win. For all these years.
No more.
You will not take my freedom away from me for another second.
I am strong.
I am free.
I have control now.
You won't control me any longer.
I am choosing to live again.
I am resurrecting myself.
No one will ever be the monster under my bed again.

Oftentimes, survivors have endured abuse that conditions them to be small and quiet, not disruptive, not causing a stir. It is one of the first challenges that faces a survivor—to believe in herself enough to be seen and heard.

"There is no greater sound to my ears, than the roar of a woman once silenced."

—Kristin Thomas

The Drama Triangle

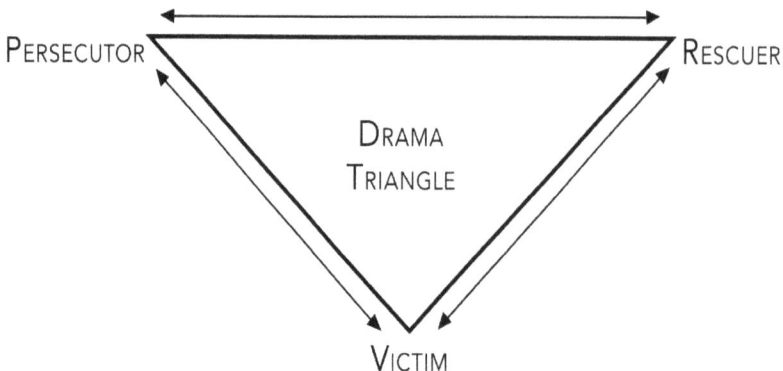

The Drama Triangle was first described by Stephen Karpman in the 1960s. It is a model of dysfunctional social interactions and illustrates a power game that involves three roles: Victim, Rescuer, and Persecutor. When we are in an abusive situation, we will play out the roles of each position many times, mistaking the change of roles as movement away from abuse. For example, Ann is the victim of severe emotional abuse from her partner Bob and her mother Jan is always trying to rescue her. But on different days Jan is actually abusive to either her daughter or Bob, and Ann becomes the "rescuer" and steps in between them. Then Bob persecutes Ann for stepping in (making her the victim). Ann then fights back making Bob the victim, her the persecutor and Jan the rescuer.

The key point is that there is no good outcome from the drama triangle, it is a trap. Once you recognize that you are caught playing any role in the drama triangle STEP OUT. Remove yourself from the whole situation, don't be tempted to rescue or you will be thrown right back into it.

> It will feel lonely and empty to begin with but it is the only way to stop the cycle you grew up with. We play in the drama triangle because it is familiar to us and there is a strange comfort in that but don't be fooled, it is a dead-end situation.

Paradox

Cassandra Sumner

Paradox—this word in all its complicity stirs thoughts from deep inside my guts. As if there are hidden worlds tucked away within the spaces of each letter. Fear, excitement, mystery, enticement, scream at me when I read the word on a seamlessly harmless page. Was this book put there for me to read that word in this moment because of the pure intensity that it would have over my life in this moment? Some might say this is a divine intervention. So quickly I find myself lost in a dark rabbit hole full of potential outcomes. Not knowing which one to trust, yet somehow, I am understanding that if I don't search and find, I could be lost forever in this cycle of only surviving.

Continuously balancing on this deathly teeter-totter of what is and what is not. Searching for the answers to why, how, and when again to be prepared. To understand the full depths of my every decision throughout my days walking on this earth. Only then will I wake up from these constant reminders of what has been, what was, and what will be.

"Just Do It" these word's play over and over in my head. Everywhere I turn I see the demanding eight letters. I see them when I fall asleep and again and again after I wake. I ask myself repeatedly until I am screaming in my head, "WHAT AM I SUPPOSED TO DO?" The feeling of pure frustration is burning from the top of my head all the way down to my feet. My eyes drift from my children's tee shirts to their eyes and I attempt to not appear in pain. I try so hard to control my facial expressions but then a quick thought appears in my mind; what if I show just a little bit of emotion to see if it triggers a twitch of a smile or a glimmer in the eyes. *Searching for some sort of confirmation that I am not making these feelings up in my head. What could be worse Cassandra, that they really have been stalking, threatening, harassing, and literally choking my very breath from lungs or that I have followed my biological fathers DNA and am officially schizophrenic?* Both scenarios cause my lungs to quickly begin to close in. I repeat to myself to breathe. In and out, in and out.

I once was afraid of the pain that came with being alone. The strength of fighting this fear has grown something greater in me than I had ever imagined. Solitude, contentment, gratitude, and trust of myself and what I will be for me. To come and go as I please, nothing holding me back or holding onto me. Was that the goal of all of this? Somehow, I can see the full circle of letting go; closing the circle, so that I can never get on this unsteady merry-go-round again.

A crystal sticking out from the ground, escaping from the mud and muck, the very substance that created it. As if it has been placed there in this very moment just for me to catch a glimpse of the shimmering layers all stacked together, creating a beautiful light.

You know what hurts the most?

That I have not yet learned how not to be hurt….

·······

Measuring Up

Candice Campo

Finally unrolled, nervous, laid out
and glared at.
"Oh, no! That printed rug
has an imperfection alongside its border.
You can hide it under the couch! Let's rotate it."

"No," she said softly, shaking her head with a smile.
"It's one of a kind. Let it breathe freely, gain confidence… an understanding that it too can hold up the world just as it came."

Recovery

RMae

There's no love left here, only a void that lingers.
Things seem to move fast once your callouses are discovered,
from all tha mental stingers.
I started to plot my escape tha first time my face caught
tha back side of his fingers...

Across my face...
Penetrated my bubble space.
Light headed, adrenaline rush, my heart begins to race.
Fight or flight, my thoughts can't keep tha pace.
Assumptions are re-victimizing, thoughts "it should be easy;
call police, restraining orders, self-defense with guns or mace!"
You have no idea! Tha grooming and narcissistic demand
that's taken place!
Tha crawling back, begging with fake tears
that are supposed to erase...

Tha scars they delt.
Physical and tha heart felt.
Seems I'd rather take tha first, than an emotional welt.
Tolerance becomes tha norm, chest tightening,
squeezing like tha notches on a belt.

Time doesn't heal or make you forget, especially
when they still haunt your every move.
Their ego is stripped they've got allot to prove.
They NEVER sacrifice, if to them it don't behoove.

It takes a while to recover
from all tha normal things they disapproved.

Please know, you can and will get your power back.
Keep fighting for your life & sanity
even when there's no one there to catch tha slack.
God made you & you're worth it,
no matter how many odds are stacked!

CHAPTER V

I walk down another street.

—Portia Nelson.

You Are Not Alone ~Rebecca Smith

SPIRIT

Jade Rosina McCutcheon

There's a storyline
path like
gossamer thread
infinite grace
delicately suspended
between daffodils
and magic
divine fine
thread
that ties
my life
to
this earth.

SINGLE

Summer Harlan

I'm here alone, yet, surrounded by life

Children wrap their loving arms around me
Animals cuddle me
Family cares about me

I'm here alone, yet, surrounded by life

People want to work with me
Students can't wait to see me
Neighbors spend their time watching me

I'm here alone, yet, surrounded by life.

Triggers and Healing

Cassandra Sumner

My 10-year-old daughter has begun experimenting with cussing with a friend through text messaging. Of course, this is a normal process of growing up but once I read this text it activated something strongly in me.

I immediately went to my daughter and told her that this kind of language is not acceptable and although I understand that she cannot control what comes out of her friend's mouth. I told my daughter she will be role modeling for her friend and not cuss. End of story.

After the conversation ended, I felt myself began to wonder why I had the need to teach her this so strongly. And how I did not give her time to explain but only acted on my triggered emotions.

After digging deeper, I was able to recognize the trigger; growing up my father would yell and cuss a lot; I was afraid of being like him. I witnessed numerous abuse situations with my mother and boyfriends and violence, yelling, and cussing were present. I was able to connect cussing to these same feelings as a little child.

I then went to my daughter and apologized. I talked to her about my personal experiences with cussing and explained that now that I am aware of this connection, I want to talk more about how her experimentation is completely normal. It was wrong of me to shame her due to my strong emotions. I have not yet fully healed. I explained the importance of a time and a place and the respect of others, because just like me, you never know who you might trigger with the words you are using.

Ending the second conversation was completely different than the first conversation with my daughter. During the second conversation my daughter was engaged, making eye contact, and laughing with me at the thought of it being okay to cuss with boundaries. I was able to thank her for being respectful of me during the times that she was talking to her friend on the phone and gave her friend direction when I would walk into the room. This was her way of protecting her friend. The shame that I originally put on her was gone. Where during the first conversation it was me telling her and a sense of deep shame; this is not the way that I hope to teach and parent. To find this balance between boundaries and teaching is so crucial for raising strong, independent children. Because as I know from personal experiences the shame from a parental figure will be carried with them until it bleeds into almost every choice they make and every direction they take.

Hindsight

Summer Harlan

When did I drink the Kool-Aid?
lose sight of truth?
disconnect from reality?

I was a child
now I am capable
watch me grow.

Watch me succeed with my children
beside me.

Secure in our new reality.

Connected to truth.

Detoxing the bullshit.

Be Kind-not Nice, Rebecca Smith

It's very easy for survivors of abuse to over-compensate and to put more worth on another person's feelings than their own. This is just a habit. You can break it. Ask yourself how YOU are today. What would YOU like to do. Even if it's only 5 or 10 minutes. Do something just for you every day and that will help to change the habit.

Roots

Jade Rosina McCutcheon

I am standing on dry land
I can help you from here
it is no good
if I jump into the sea with you.

We might drown each other
thrashing our arms
trying to keep heads
above water.

My feet are like roots into the ground
I can guide you back
shout your name
shine a light.

Remind you what earth
looks like, feels like—
you don't have to be lost
at sea forever.

Sentinel ~Jade Rosina McCutcheon

New Growth

Cassandra Sumner

I heard my name in the echoes.
I was fighting the mud, stuck in the undertows.

Like a lamp for my ears, I knew I was near.
Straining each time I broke free to hear.

Your strong roots are safely in place.
A beacon in this dark and confusing space.

I can see you now.
I am learning how.

I can feel the dry land, and you reach out your hand.

I will add to the loudness of the light.
To shine the names of all still lost in the night.

SECTION TWO

HEALTHY RELATIONSHIP BEHAVIORS & DYNAMICS

I Will Protect You ~Jarmac

Take care of your wounded child, she doesn't need to be beat up and criticized any more.

The Good Mother Exercise

This exercise is an approach I have shared with many survivors over the years. Like most things it is a compilation of experience and teachings from different cultures, different women I have learned from and many healers. There are many approaches to healing after trauma, this exercise can be used with a variety of other approaches.

Early Childhood Trauma

We each carry within us, a pattern of the abuse we received as children. Many psychology approaches believe that the period between 0 -5 or 0 -7 years is the most formative and therefore key to understanding what is driving our negative patterns and behaviors. In that period, we receive data like a little computer, without realizing it, our parents are programming us, usually with the way they were raised. These programs are stored away in our brain like sets of instructions about how to react to life, how to survive, how to interact with others, how to communicate.

As children we are very "programmable," we watch everything and learn from those around us. Our parents are the key inputs when we are very little and we tend to mimic their behaviors. If our upbringing was violent or abusive then we tend to be drawn to others with the same behaviors and wounds.

When there is violence and trauma in our childhood, these programs become set in our brain and body in a way that other programs do not. Extreme trauma affects the brain in such a way that we are not able to think clearly in response to similar trauma later on in life.

> "... when the brain repeatedly interprets danger (trauma), it can *shut off* the connection to the "thinking brain" and an individual might feel like their brain is alerting them to danger all the time, even when the 'thinking brain' tells them a person or situation is safe."
>
> —Jade Rosina McCutcheon

Alright, so we might know that we are dealing with a traumatized part of the self but how do we heal that? How do we manage it?

THE GOOD MOTHER AND THE WOUNDED CHILD

The Good Mother Exercise is based on the realization that a wounded child is running our life and sometimes we feel out of control and unable to reach the part of us that seems "out of control." The damaging program we received as a child has not been amended, has not been addressed or re-written and so it is wired into the hard data, and it's been there for so long we don't know how to find it.

I've often described the power of the wounded child as something like this: You are the captain of a ship on its way to a beautiful island. You are going there for some much-needed rest and relaxation. As captain you feel pretty sure everything is in order but suddenly the ship starts turning around and heading to another destination. The engine is sputtering and it seems as though you've lost control. This is the wounded child in the engine room, sabotaging everything down there, pushing buttons and pulling levers, creating mayhem.

This is the power of our emotions when we are triggered by a situation and our response is a trauma response. We shut down, go into "flight or fright" or experience deep anxiety and panic.

The Good Mother Exercise is to find that wounded child and talk to her, no matter how scared or unsure you are. This is the work; this is the path to getting back behind the wheel and steering your life in the way you want to steer it. It's a long journey, it can take years, but it is rewarding and real. That little girl (I'm using the female gender because overwhelmingly women are in the majority as victims of violence), has been beaten up and discarded. The habit of beating on her has been instilled in you. It's easy to put yourself down, blame yourself, that's what you were taught as a child.

> Here are some tips for creating and maintaining a healthy relationship with yourself and others.
>
> - Allow space to make mistakes/open communication.
> - Taking time together and time for yourself.
> - A partner who wants you to do well/to grow independently.
> - Explore unconditional expressions of love or affection. Not requiring gifts or any action from the other.

- Honesty/Trust.
- Allow each other to be different, with different value systems. Listen to each other's opinions even if different.
- Create a safe and supportive environment.

Trauma Impacts and Resilience

To better understand how survivors respond to trauma, it is important to have a basic understanding of the brain and how trauma affects the brain.

Parts of the Brain

Brain Stem
- Takes care of the most basic things (breathing, making your heart beat)

Limbic (Lizard) Brain
- Takes in sensory information (sights, sounds, tastes, smells, sensations)
- Decides if you are in danger
- Starts the "Freeze, Fight, or Flight" reaction
- Helps you manage emotions including fear
- Takes short-term memories and moves them to long term memory storage

Neocortex
- Your thinking brain: complex problem solving and higher thinking, interpreting situations and emotions happen here.

Fight, Flight, or Freeze

First, the limbic (lizard) brain receives sensory info and decides if you are in danger.

If it decides you are in danger, the *fight, flight, or freeze pathway* turns on because it is faster than the neocortex or thinking brain pathway.

If danger is repeated often, this pathway remains open/on. And when the brain repeatedly interprets danger (trauma), it can shut off the connection to the "thinking brain."

You might feel:
- ... like your brain is alerting you to danger all the time, even when the "thinking brain" tells you a person or situation is safe.

- ... or that you are not in danger, even when the "thinking brain" is telling you that something or someone is very risky.
- ... unsure about how you are feeling.
- ... overwhelmed by emotions or extremely fearful.
- ... numb or as though you can't feel things very deeply.

The "lizard" brain remembers what it was seeing, hearing, smelling, tasting, and touching when it decided you were in danger. These sensory memories can get stuck in this part of the brain and become triggers or cause nightmares.

Trauma memories can also get stuck in short-term memory storage. Instead of being processed and filed under "past things that happened," a person with a trauma memory *may continue to experience it as though it just happened* (like a short-term memory) every time it comes into their mind. This may be the case even many years later.

How Trauma Can Affect Survivors:

- It is normal for survivors to have difficulty accessing memories.
- Stories may change or appear made up if we aren't aware of how trauma affects the brain and memories.

- Each time the story is re-told, it will trigger and re-traumatize the survivor. This can make their appearances in court—or with police or other authority figures—seem less reliable.
- Triggers are things or events that cause an individual to re-experience trauma.
- These could include scents, textures, words, colors, objects, and more.
- Triggers can cause stress responses without the survivor knowing or being able to explain.

Dissociation
- Dissociation is a lack of connection to the current events.
- Dissociation is created by the brain.
- For example, a mild form of dissociation can occur when you are driving and realize that you can't remember the last few miles on the highway.

- In its most severe form, dissociation can manifest as multiple personalities.
- Dissociation allows somebody experiencing a traumatic event to effectively not be present; to "go somewhere else" in their mind to keep them safe.
- Humans will focus inherently on their most urgent or highest need, or what they perceive that to be. During times of trauma that may not be the current reality.
- It may be safer or more important for the brain to shift its focus, resulting in dissociation.
- We dissociate every day, but survivors do it on a much more frequent basis and to a larger degree.

PHYSICAL HEALTH EFFECTS OF TRAUMA:
- Heart issues
- Gastro-intestinal, IBS
- Headaches
- Diabetes
- Chronic remembering of daily experiences or tasks
- Chronic pain
- Fibromyalgia

BRAIN CHANGES:
- Adrenaline changes: an increase of adrenaline is normal in response to danger, and the surge dies down when the danger is gone.
- But cumulative trauma may cause the adrenaline surge to have trouble turning off, or it may limit the ability of the adrenaline to appear when the individual is in danger.
- Hormonal alterations: Similar to adrenaline, hormones such as cortisol are released in response to stressful situations. Trauma can cause these hormones to be released in amounts that are greater than or less than the optimal amount.
- Trauma can reduce the size of the parts of the brain that process memory and regulate emotion.
- Trauma can increase activity of the limbic brain, resulting in changes to the individual's ability to regulate their emotions.

> But trauma can have positive impacts on survivors as well.

SURVIVAL SKILLS:
- Awareness of danger — "Traumavision!"
- Ability to care for, soothe, or placate even dangerous others
- Ability to endure: pain, hurt, loss, fear
- Ability to recognize and interrupt cycles of trauma that often cross generations, or to protect their children the way they may not have been protected
- Potential to help other survivors

FACTORS THAT CAN *INCREASE THE RISK OF NEGATIVE SYMPTOMS* IN REACTION TO TRAUMA:
- Severe, repeated traumatic events
- Early childhood trauma
- Poverty
- Parents who had Post Traumatic Stress Disorder (PTSD)
- Family history of psychiatric problems
- Pre-existing psychiatric symptoms/diagnosis
- Prior trauma
- Life stressors.

FACTORS THAT REDUCE THE RISK OF NEGATIVE SYMPTOMS:
- Ability to help or protect others at the time of the traumatic event
- Support network (people, organizations, churches, online, etc.)
- Education (about trauma, PTSD, and coping)
- Resources (financial, family, creative, personal, emotional, etc.)
- Belief system — religious or not, an ability to make meaning out of the experience

HEALTHY COPING:
- Routines
- Healthy eating & sleeping

- Mindfulness
- Exercise
- Self-pacing
- Inspirations
- Support
- Self-compassion
- Creativity

Healing from Trauma

- In the beginning, safety is what's most important. <u>Increase safety</u>, both the external safety of people and environment, and internal, emotional safety.
- After reaching safety, a person may choose to engage in remembrance and mourning.

Power & Control

Abuse is about power and control but how do we understand power? Words like manipulation, gaslighting, violence and narcissism are used often around domestic and sexual violence to describe the nature of the abuse or abuser. The bottom line is that the abusive person wants power over the other, they want to control them and make them do what they want rather than develop respect and communication skills that would allow both people in the relationship to prosper and have equal say.

Sometimes it's because there is a different expectation about what marriage is, sometimes it's due to cultural differences and sometimes it's the way the abuser was raised.

Survivor Account

L was married at seventeen to a man from a different culture who was raised to expect his wife to always be in the kitchen, clean the house, cook the dinners, look after the kids and to never talk back. While they were dating, he was charming and generous, even romantic. As soon as they were married, he began to behave as though he owned her. She began to talk back and tried to tell him she didn't want to be an obedient pet; she wanted her own life too. He began hitting her and isolating her from her friends and family. His family expected her to behave in the same way and his mother told her to just accept it. She ended up in the hospital several times but was too afraid to leave him. Her husband was seeing other women, staying out late and beating her often.

She had no money or transportation and her kids depended on her. Her family wasn't speaking to her and she had no energy to resist anymore. When we use the word "survivor," it's important to understand just what this woman has been through and how incredibly hard it is to make it out of that dark place. What surprises me is the generosity and warmth of the survivors I have met, when they have every right to be bitter, broken, and angry.

Abuse is about POWER and CONTROL. We often don't see the signs when we fall in love. Dynamics can change when women become pregnant; partners can become abusive and angry. They often feel "left out" of love because the mother is so busy with the baby and so they act out against the woman thinking she is rejecting him. If young men were taught about responsible fatherhood in schools this situation might not occur to the degree it does now. When the husband feels he has lost control of his wife's love and consequently her behavior towards him, he tries to regain that control physically. Understanding what it takes to raise children should be part of the curriculum in every school.

> "The Power and Control Wheel was created in 1982 by Ellen Pence, Coral McDonnell, and Michael Paymar as part of a curriculum for a court ordered program for men who batter. It was developed out of the experiences of women who were battered and attending support and educational groups in the working-class town of Duluth, Minnesota. These women were asked, 'What do you want taught in court ordered groups for men who batter?'
>
> "Their answers spoke to the need to bring the complex reality of battering out into the open. That is, the lived experience of what actually goes on in a battering relationship needed to be recognized and exposed. As the designers probed, women began to talk about the tactics their partners used to control them. Violence was commonplace. Less recognized but equally significant were other tactics of power, *including money, the children, emotional and psychological put downs, undermining self-worth and other social relationships, constant criticism of women's mothering, intimidation and various forms of expressing male privilege.*
>
> "The wheel is not a theory. It is a conceptual tool. It helps people see the patterns in behavior and their significance. It is not intended to capture every tactic of control, just primary tactics. Nor will all empirical cases correspond exactly to the wheel. The wheel was based on women's experience in hetero-sexual intimate partner relationships. The battered women did not identify a desire for power or control as motivating their partners to engage in these behaviors. Rather, men who batter gained power and control in the relationship as an outcome of those behaviors."
>
> —Domestic Intervention Programs, Duluth, MN

When we consider the many ways in which one person can exert power over another, I think we can all relate. Abuse of power is rife in our culture; at what point do we say no? At what point do we walk away, especially when we have children and no money.

What is Gaslighting?

You know that you are self-aware. You have strong opinions, defined goals, and at the core, you know who you are. Then one day, seemingly out of nowhere, you begin doubting things, questioning people's motives, second-guessing what you want and who you are. Your confidence turns to suspicion. You feel neurotic and paranoid. You may even start to wonder, "Am I going crazy?"

You're not crazy.

Gaslighting is a manipulative tactic in which a person, to gain power and control, plants seeds of uncertainty in the victim. The self-doubt and constant skepticism slowly and meticulously create an atmosphere where the individual begins question their reality. Gaslighting is a form of mental and emotional abuse. It promotes anxiety, depression, and can trigger mental breakdowns.

Perhaps the best way to examine this inherently abusive behavior is to go straight to the source, the 1944 film *Gaslight*. The film tells a story of a husband systematically brainwashing his wife to the point that she thinks she is going insane. The wife fights to protect her identity all while her husband viciously tries to take it away.

One of the most troubling aspects of gaslighting is that everyone is at risk. In fact, it is a method commonly used by cult leaders and dictators. While, many of us have the good sense to not join a cult, we can experience gaslighting in our personal relationships without even realizing it. Furthermore, gaslighting happens in a deliberately slow, precise way to ensure that the victim doesn't realize it's even happening.

It's hard to recognize this type of abuse because in addition to lying, the gaslighter may also be incredibly charming. At first, you may even find yourself feeling guilty that you are second-guessing this person. Quickly you begin ignoring your gut. This confusion is precisely what the abuser wants. As a result, without even realizing it, you are in an abusive relationship.

I Don't Know Who I Am Anymore ~Jarmac

Examples of Gaslighting

Are you a victim of gaslighting manipulation? Take a look at the following tell-tale signs of gaslighting behavior:

1. Blatant Lying

First, people who gaslight tell obvious lies. You know that they are lying. The issue is how they are lying with such ease. The gaslighter is setting up an abusive pattern. You begin to question everything and become uncertain of the simplest matters. This self-doubt is exactly what the gaslighter wants.

2. Deny, Deny, Deny

Again, *you know* they said what they said, however, they completely deny ever saying it. The gaslighter may push the point and ask you to "prove it," knowing that you only have your memory of the conversation. It starts to make you question your memory and your reality. You begin to wonder if the gaslighter is right, maybe they didn't really ever say what you remember. Consequently, more and more often, you question your reality and accept theirs.

3. Using What You Love Against You

Additionally, people who gaslight use what is closest to you against you. If you love your job, they will find issues with it. If you have children, the gaslighter may force you to believe you should never have had them. This abusive manipulation tactic causes the victim to question the foundation of themselves as well as what they hold close.

4. The Slow Death of Self

One of the terrifying parts of gaslighting is the methodical timeline that the abuser uses. The manipulation happens gradually and over time the victim morphs into someone entirely different. The most confident human being can become a shell of a person without being aware of it in the process. The victim's individual reality diminishes and becomes that of the abuser.

5. Words vs. Actions

Notably, a person who gaslights talks and talks. However, their words have no meaning, therefore, it is important to look at their actions. The issues lie in their abusive actions towards the victim.

6. Love and Flattery

A common technique of a person who gaslights is to tear you down and then build you back up, only to tear you down again. Whether you realize it or not, you are becoming used to being torn down. However, the praise may lead you to think that the abuser isn't all that bad.

7. Confusion

Without a doubt, people crave stability, and the gaslighter knows this. The constant confusion that the abuser has instilled leads the victim to become desperate for clarity. More often than not, the victim searches for this clarity in the abuser, thus continuing the cycle and increasing the power that the abuser has.

8. Projecting

If the gaslighter is a liar and a cheater, they are now accusing you of being a liar and a cheater. You constantly feel like you need to defend yourself for things you haven't done.

9. "You're crazy"

The gaslighter knows you are already questioning your sanity. The gaslighter also knows that you search for clarity in the person who is purposefully causing the confusion. Therefore, when they call you crazy, you believe it.

Furthermore, the gaslighter may also tell other people that you're crazy. This way if you were ever to approach them for help with your abuser, they wouldn't believe you. The gaslighter has given them a heads up that this would happen. You're too "crazy" to be taken seriously.

10. Everyone Else is a Liar

The abuser may also tell you that everyone else is against you and that they are all liars. Again, believing that everyone else is lying to you forces your sense of reality to be further blurred. People who gaslight want their victims to turn to them for everything so that they can continue the abuse.

NAVIGATING THE LEGAL SYSTEM

SURVIVOR ACCOUNT

After calling her sister to her bring her a bra and a pair of shoes to the safe house she was at, S headed to the courthouse to file a restraining order (RO). She had left last night in her pajamas, both she and son barefoot. After getting the packet of forms to fill out, S had a hard time calming her hand enough to write her name. Her sister took the pen from her hand, and started reading out the questions; "My name, my address …. His name, his address." And then she arrived at the question, "Describe what happened." There were maybe a few lines of space available on the paper, and S thought, "How do I write what happened last night into that small space? How do I communicate the fear, the terror, the devastation my son witnessed? How do I condense it to fit these few lines?"

It was the first of many times, S would be marginalized and minimized as a survivor.

ADVICE FROM OREGON ATTORNEY, DAVID JOHNSON

(INTERVIEW BY KRISTIN THOMAS)

Thomas: What is the average cost to retain an attorney for a restraining order case in Marion and Polk counties?

Johnson: The average cost to retain an attorney on a restraining order is between $1,500 and $4,000. Many attorneys will do restraining order hearings on a flat fee, meaning once you have paid the retainer you are done paying.

Thomas: What are some of the most common reasons for a restraining order to be dismissed at trial?

Johnson: There are two common reasons restraining orders get dismissed:

1. The petition for the restraining order did not contain sufficient information about the abuse.
2. Victims lack documentation of the abuse.

Thomas: In your experience, what advice would you give a survivor of domestic violence navigating the legal system?

Johnson: It is not cost effective to have an attorney help you obtain the restraining order. Victims can do that without legal assistance.

- When filling out the petition for the restraining order, list all instances of abuse and detail the physical and emotional injuries. If the restraining order is contested victims are limited to the instances that are contained in the petition and cannot describe additional acts at the time of trial.
- Take photographs of bruises, cuts, broken items.
- Report the abuse to law enforcement in all cases and medical professionals as appropriate.
- If your restraining order is contested, then hire an attorney.

Survivor Account

J was granted a temporary restraining order by a female interim judge in her county. She had asked that her abuser be ordered to leave the home they shared, so she could return. It was granted. She was staying at a safe house with her child, and really wanted to go back home where things were familiar for her child. After about 5 days of waiting to be notified by the Sheriff's office that her abuser had been served and removed from the home, she went to the Sheriff's office after dropping her child off at school. She was informed that he had not been served, and that there was no restraining order in their system under his name. J showed the clerk the signed copy of the restraining order she received from the judge. The clerk looked at the judge's signature and said, "There is no judge in this county by that name." J was shocked! She had been in court, spoke to the judge, and watched her sign the order!! Was this clerk calling her a liar? The conversation was overheard by another clerk, who took J into their office to talk. After checking the computer, this clerk apologized profusely to J and said that yes, the restraining order was there, and that it would be served ASAP.

When filing for a restraining order, attach as many pages as needed to capture as many instances of the abuse you suffered as possible. If it is not listed, the judge won't consider it as evidence.

For more information about filing a restraining order in Oregon, visit:
courts.oregon.gov/programs/family/domestic-violence/Pages/restraining.aspx

Uprooting

As a victim of domestic and/or sexual abuse—

You are NOT:
- To blame
- Less Than
- Not worthy
- Broken beyond repair
- Crazy
- Overreacting
- In any way responsible

You ARE:
- A survivor
- Strong
- Brave
- Doing the best you can in the moment
- Breathing
- Healing
- Growing
- Learning

Uprooting is hard, but you can do it!

Yes, it IS hard! It's downright terrifying at times! The life you have been living, or are still living in, while abusive, is familiar. And making the decision to live your life safe from the monsters in it, will force you into a terrifying new place; the unknown. You might learn that leaving may have been the easiest part. It's the staying gone and healing that might test every ounce of your faith, drain you of every resource, and challenge your endurance. It will challenge you as a woman, a friend, a sister and a mother to own your rightful place in this universe, and to exercise your primal right to protect your children.

You WILL get there and the result from choosing to walk down the other street, is to find the most beautiful, free, loving place you could ever imagine. It is full of thousands of women who went before you, who made the journey. Those women are your sisters, your mentors, your safe place; find them, we are here.

There Will Be Days

Shawn Aveningo Sanders

A trigger will transport you
where you didn't plan to go—

    Scent of juniper
        wafting from your in-law's hedge
        while visiting their mountain home.
            You recall gin is made from juniper berries,
            which reminds you of sloe gin,
            and then you remember
                    the smell of his breath.

    The accidental scrape of fingernail
        against a crisp, white-linen tablecloth
        elicits synaptic electricity,
        a snap.
            And suddenly,
            it's your fingernails scraping
            the bedsheet, clawing the dark
                    trying to escape.

    Careless Whisper
        plays on the car radio,
        and as much as you love George Michael
        you change the station.
            This song a painful reminder
            of that empty bottle of sleeping pills
            and the belief
                you're never gonna dance again.

But there will be many days
when happiness persists—

The wonder in your son's eyes
        meeting his twin baby sisters.
        How he slips into that big brother role
        in an instant,
                picking up a baby bottle
                to help with the feeding,
                      and you kiss his tiny blonde head.

The cleverness of twin little girls,
        the night they move a mattress
        into the hallway outside your bedroom,
        perhaps to be closer to you,
        perhaps just to prove they can.
                You trip over the mess
                ready to scold them,
                their giggles become contagious,
                      and you can't help but join the laughter.

There will be
        home runs / blue ribbons / birthdays
        family reunions / weddings / graduations
        school plays / prom dresses / soccer games
        old friends / new friends / celebrations
        new jobs / new houses / promotions
        new dreams / new life / new loves
                      and Grandchildren!

and through it all
        you will re-discover yourself,
        your purpose, your essence, your sexuality,
        and finally realize
                how beautiful you are,
                how strong you always have been,
                and how to accept love
                      from a man who never once asked
                              what you were wearing.

Flowering ~Jade Rosina McCutcheon

We sincerely hope this collection of art, poetry and personal stories conveys our intention of lifting domestic and sexual abuse out of the darkness and into light.

Resources for Finding Help

The resources listed on the next few pages are ready and available to you.

National Resources

National Domestic Violence Hotline

24-hour Crisis Hotline: (800) 799-SAFE (7233)
Website: thehotline.org
24 hours a day, seven days a week, 365 days a year, the National Domestic Violence Hotline provides essential tools and support to help survivors of domestic violence so they can live their lives free of abuse. Highly trained, expert advocates offer free, confidential, and compassionate support, crisis intervention information, education, and referral services in over 200 languages.

National Domestic Abuse Intervention Program

Phone: (737) 225-3150 (administrative)
24-hour Crisis Hotline: (800) 799-7233

PAVE (Promoting Awareness | Victim Empowerment)

Website: shatteringthesilence.org
PAVE supports and empowers victim-survivors and strives to prevent sexual violence through education, advocacy, and community action.

RAINN (Rape, Abuse & Incest National Network)

24-hour Crisis Hotline: (800) 656-HOPE (4673)
Website: rainn.org
RAINN is the nation's largest anti-sexual violence organization. RAINN created and operates the National Sexual Assault Hotline in partnership with more than 1,000 local sexual assault service providers across the country and operates the DoD Safe Helpline for the Department of Defense. RAINN also carries out programs to prevent sexual violence, help survivors, and ensure that perpetrators are brought to justice.

Survivors.org

Search for shelters, support organizations, and services in the United States. Specific filtered seach pages for the following areas of concern:
Childhood Abuse webpage: survivors.org/childhood-trauma
Domestic Violence webpage: survivors.org/domestic-violence
Sexual Abuse webpage: survivors.org/sexual-violence

Resources in Oregon

Abby's House at Western Oregon University
Phone: (503) 838-8219
Website: wou.edu/abbyshouse
Provides the Western Oregon University (WOU) community with educational programming, information, and referral services designed to promote equity and non-violence. They embrace a feminist model that empowers all people to actively stand against all forms of violence, harassment, verbal abuse, discrimination, and hatred.

Bradley Angle
Counties Served: Multnomah
Phone: (503) 232-1528
24-hour crisis and support hotline, support groups, confidential and legal advocacy, services for children and youth, confidential advocacy, safety planning, emergency shelter, transitional housing, and referrals to other services. Healing Roots Program (culturally specific services for the African American community); LGBTQ program; HIV-positive survivors.

Bridges of Oregon
Address: 1115 Madison St. NE, #1069, Salem, OR 97301
Phone: (971) 202-1500 (main) | (971) 800-6250 (advocate)
Email: info@bridgesoregon.org
Provides advocacy services.

Call to Safety
Counties Served: Multnomah, Washington
Phone: (503) 235-5333
24-hour crisis and support hotline, and referrals to other services, support groups, confidential and legal advocacy, safety planning, and referrals to other services.

Canyon Crisis and Resource Centre
Servicing: Rural communities of North Santiam Canyon - Mill City, Oregon
Phone: (503) 897-2327
Email: ccrisisc@gmail.com

Center Against Rape and Domestic Violence
24-hour Crisis & Support Line: (541) 754-0110 or (800) 927-0197
Main Office: (541) 758-0219

Center for Hope and Safety

Counties Served: Marion, Polk
Address: 605 Center St. NE, Salem, OR 97301
24-hour hotline: (503) 399-7722 | toll free: (866) 399-7722
Main Office Phone: (503) 378-1572
24-hour crisis and support hotline, support groups, confidential and legal advocacy, services for children and youth, safety planning, emergency shelter, transitional housing, prevention education, and referrals to other services.

Child Abuse Hotline

Counties Served: Polk, Marion, Yamhill
Phone: (855) 503-7233
Open to anyone who would like to report concerns of child abuse or neglect.

Clackamas Women's Services: A Safe Place Family Justice Center

Address: 256 Warner Milne Rd., Oregon City, OR 97045
24-hour Crisis & Support Line: (888) 654-2288
Phone: (503) 655-8600

Community Works

Counties Served: Jackson
Address: 2594 E. Barnett Rd., Suite C, Medford, OR 97504
Help Line (541) 779.4357, Office: (541) 779.2393
Español: (541) 779-2393, ext. 209

Confederated Tribes of Grand Ronde: "Warriors of Hope" DV Services

Address: 9615 Grand Ronde Road, Grand Ronde, OR 97347
Phone: (503) 879-5211
Crisis Hotline: (971) 241-3594

Confederated Tribes of Siletz Indians: CARE Program

Counties Served: Lane, Lincoln
Phone: (541) 444 9680
24-hour crisis and support hotline, and referrals to other services, Support groups, Legal advocacy, Services for children and youth, Confidential advocacy, safety planning, and referrals to other services.

Coquille Indian Tribe

Counties Served: Coos, Lane, Jackson, Curry
Phone: (541) 756-0904
Legal advocacy, prevention education, confidential advocacy, safety planning, referrals to other services

Department of Domestic Services

Counties Served: Yamhill
Address: 368 NE Norton Ln, McMinnville, OR
Phone: (503) 472 0311

Disability Rights Oregon

Counties Served: All
Address: 511 SW 10th Ave., Suite 200, Portland, Oregon 97205
Phone: (503) 243-2081
Email: welcome@droregon.org

Domestic Violence Resource Center

Counties Served: Washington
Address: 9320 SW Barbur Blvd., Suite #250, Portland, OR 97219
Phone: (503) 230-1951
Phone: (503) 640-5352, ext. 143
Crisis Hotline: (503) 469-8620
Support groups, legal advocacy, legal representation and advice, services for children and youth, counseling and therapy services, confidential advocacy, safety planning, prevention education, hospital response for sexual assault survivors, emergency shelter, and referrals to other services.

Domestic Violence Services

Counties Served: Morrow, Umatilla
Phone: (541) 276-3322
Support groups, legal advocacy, legal representation and advice, services for children and youth, counseling and therapy services, confidential advocacy, safety planning, prevention education, hospital response for sexual assault survivors, accompaniment to court with survivors, and referrals to other services.

El Programa Hispano Católico

Counties Served: Multnomah
Address: 333 SE 223rd Ave, Portland, OR 97030
Phone: (503) 688-2631 or (503) 669-8350

Family Building Blocks, Dallas

Counties Served: Polk
Address: 182 SW Academy St., Dallas, OR 97338
Phone: (503) 623 9664
Website: www.familybuildingblocks.org
Provides parenting classes, prenatal and family parenting.

Family Building Blocks, Salem

Helen's Place: 180 18th St., Salem OR 97301
Phone: (503) 798 4744
www.familybuildingblocks.org

Gateway Center for DV Services

Counties Served: Multnomah
Address: 9320 SW Barbur Blvd., Suite #250, Portland, OR 97219
Phone: (503) 988-6400
Crisis Hotline: (503) 235-5333
Support groups, legal advocacy, legal representation and advice, services for children and youth, counseling and therapy services, confidential advocacy, safety planning, and referrals to other services.

Grand Ronde Domestic & Sexual Violence Prevention Program

Counties Served: Polk, Yamhill
Phone: (503) 879-1660
For all Grand Ronde tribal members, community, and staff.

Harney Hope

Counties Served: Harney
Address: 85 N Date Street, Burns OR 97720
Phone: (541) 573-2726
Crisis Hotline: (541) 573-7176
24-hour crisis and support hotline, and referrals to other services, emergency shelter, support groups, prevention education, confidential advocacy, safety planning, and referrals to other services.

HAVEN from Domestic and Sexual Violence

Counties Served: Gilliam, Sherman, Wasco, Wheeler
Address: 420 E. 3rd Street, The Dalles, OR 97058
Phone: (541) 296-1662
Crisis Hotline: (800) 249-4789
24-hour crisis and support hotline, emergency shelter, transitional housing, support groups, legal advocacy, economic justice and financial advocacy, services for children and youth, prevention education, counseling and therapy services, confidential advocacy, safety planning, and referrals to other services.

Head Start of Yamhill County

Address: 1006 NE 3rd St., Suite A, McMinnville OR
Phone: (503) 472-2000
Website: www.yamhillheadstart.org
Family parenting classes.

Heart of Grant County

Counties Served: Grant
Address: 115 NW Bridge St., John Day, OR 97845
Phone: (541) 575-4335

Helping Hands Against Violence

Counties Served: Hood River
Address: 9320 SW Barbur Blvd., Suite #250, Portland, OR 97219
Phone: (541) 386-4808
24-hour crisis and support hotline, emergency shelter, transitional housing, support groups, legal advocacy, economic justice and financial advocacy, services for children and youth, prevention education, counseling and therapy services, confidential advocacy, safety planning, and referrals to other services.

Henderson House

Counties Served: Yamhill
Address: 610 SE First St., McMinnville, OR 97128
Phone: (503) 472-1503, ext. 302
Crisis Hotline: (503) 472-1503
24-hour crisis and support hotline, emergency shelter, support groups, services for children and youth, prevention education, confidential advocacy, safety planning, and referrals to other services.

Hope and Safety Alliance

Counties Served: Lane
Address: 1577 Pearl Street, 2nd Floor, Eugene, OR 97401
Crisis Line: (541) 485-6513
Office: (541) 485-8232

Illinois Valley Safe House Alliance

Counties Served: Josephine
Address: 103 South Kerby Ave., Cave Junction, OR. 97523 (Next to DMV)
Phone: (541) 592-2515
Crisis Hotline: (541) 415-9367

Impact NW: Parent Child Therapeutic Services

Counties Served: Multnomah
Phone: (503) 721-6776
Services for children and youth, prevention education, confidential advocacy, safety planning, counseling and therapy services, and referrals to other services.

IRCO-Refugee and Immigrant Family Strengthening

Address: 9320 SW Barbur Blvd., Suite 250, Portland, OR 97219
Phone: (503) 230-1951
Languages Spoken: English, French, German, Hindi, Hmong, Portuguese, Russian, Spanish, Ukrainian, Urdu, Vietnamese.
Support groups, legal advocacy, economic justice and financial advocacy, services for children and youth, confidential advocacy, safety planning, and referrals to other services.

Jackson County SART

Phone: (541) 441-3596 or (541) 625-8089
Email: vrs.sart@outlook.com
Confidential advocacy, safety planning, and referrals to other services.

Juliette's House

Counties Served: Polk, Yamhill
Address: 1075 SE Cedarwood Ave, McMinnville, OR
Phone: (503) 435-1550
Child abuse exam and screening.

Klamath Advocacy Center

Office: (541) 859-8938
Crisis Line: (541) 884-0390
24-hour crisis and support hotline, confidential advocacy, safety planning, counseling and therapy services, emergency shelter, legal advocacy, support groups, transitional housing, and referrals to other services.

Lake County Crisis Center

Counties Served: Lake
Phone: (541) 947-2498
Crisis Hotline: (541) 947-2449
24-hour crisis and support hotline, confidential advocacy, economic justice and financial advocacy, emergency shelter, legal advocacy, safety planning, services for children and youth, support groups, and referrals to other services.

Lutheran Community Services Northwest

Address: 605 SE Cesar E. Chavez Blvd., Portland, OR 97214
Phone: (971) 888-7827 or (503) 231-7480
Asylum seekers, citizenship, immigration, resettlement, crime victims.

MayDay Inc.

Counties Served: Baker
Phone: (541) 523-9472

Crisis Hotline: (541) 523-4134

24-hour crisis and support hotline, confidential advocacy, counseling and therapy services, emergency shelter, legal advocacy, legal representation and advice, prevention education, safety planning, services for children and youth, support groups, and referrals to other services.

MARION COUNTY VICTIM'S ASSISTANCE

Address: 555 Court St. NE, Ste 3231, Salem, OR
Phone: (503) 588-5253
Crisis intervention, emotional support for victims of crime, information and referrals.

MY SISTER'S PLACE/MY SAFE PLACE MSP

Counties Served: Lincoln
Phone: (541) 574-9424
Crisis Hotline: (541) 994-5959
Confidential advocacy, safety planning, counseling and therapy services, 24-hour crisis and support hotline, economic justice and financial advocacy, and referrals to other services.

NAYA FAMILY CENTER (NATIVE AMERICAN YOUTH AND FAMILY CENTER)

Address: 5135 NE Columbia Blvd., Portland, OR 97218
Phone: (503) 288-8177
NAYA is committed to developing the next generation of community leadership through the Oregon LEAD program. The Portland Youth and Elders Council has provided the Native youth and elders a safe and meaningful space to identify and address issues that negatively impact the Native American and Alaska Native community. By partnering with other diverse Native and mainstream organizations, they are able to strengthen the fabric of the Native voice throughout the region.

NEW BEGINNINGS INTERVENTION CENTER

Counties Served: Lake
Phone: (541) 576-3009
Crisis Hotline: (800) 850-4838
24-hour crisis and support hotline, confidential advocacy, safety planning, emergency shelter, prevention education, services for children and youth, support groups, and referrals to other services.

NORTHWEST FAMILY SERVICES – CASA ESPERANZA

Counties Served: Clackamas
Phone: (503) 974-9882
Crisis Hotline: (503) 253-5333
Confidential advocacy, safety planning, emergency shelter, legal advocacy, services for children and youth, support groups, and referrals to other services.

NorthWest Senior and Disability Services

Counties Served: Polk, Marion, Yamhill
Hotline for reporting elderly abuse: (800) 846-9165

Oasis Advocacy & Shelter Inc.

Counties Served: Curry
Phone: (541) 425-5238
Crisis Hotline: (800) 447-1167
24-hour crisis and support hotline, confidential advocacy, safety planning, counseling and therapy services, economic justice and financial advocacy, emergency shelter, legal advocacy, support groups, and referrals to other services.

Oregon Coalition Against Domestic and Sexual Violence

Website: www.ocadsv.org/find-help/

Oregon Youth Line

Phone: (877) 968-8491
Free, confidential teen to teen crisis hotline.

Polk County Crime Victim's Assistance

Address: 850 Main St., Dallas, OR
Phone: (503) 623-9268
Advocates for victims of crime and families, court support.

Sable House

Counties Served: Polk, Marion
24-hour Crisis Hotline: (503) 623-4033
Office: (503) 623-6703
Website: sablehouse.org
Their mission is to increase the safety of domestic and sexual violence victims in Polk County through crisis intervention and community education services. Provides extensive women's crisis, domestic violence, and shelter services.

Shelter Resources in Salem, Oregon

- Salvation Army Lighthouse Shelter: (503) 585-6688 (men and women)
- Union Gospel Mission: (503) 363-3983 (men)
- Simonka Place Shelter: (503) 363-7487 (women and children, no boys over 12)
- Family Promise of the Mid-Willamette Valley: (503) 370-9752 (temporary housing for families)
- St Francis: (503) 588-0428

- St Joseph: (503) 845-6147 (Mt Angel area)
- Women of the Well-Grace House: (971) 600-3627 (women with children).
- Taylor's House: (971) 273-7300 (teens: 11-17 yrs. old, 18-yrs old if still in school)

Acknowledgments

"Autobiography in Five Short Chapters" is from *There's a Hold in My Sidewalk: The Romance of Self-Discovery* by Portia Nelson. Copyright © 1993 by Portia Nelson. Reprinted with the permission of Beyond Words/Atria Books, a division of Simon & Schuster, Inc. All Rights Reserved.

The Power & Control Wheel was created Ellen Pence, Coral McDonnell, and Michael Paymar. Copyright ©1982 by Domestic Abuse Intervention Program. Reprinted with permission from Judy Breuer from the Domestic Abuse Intervention Program (202 East Superior St., Duluth, MN.55802, (218) 722-2781).

The following poems by our contributors were first published in the following journals, anthologies, or single author poetry collections:

"Matryoshka" by Dale Champlin, *Voices of Eve* (Issue 7, May 2018)

"Facedown" by Sherri Levine, *CALYX*, Winner of the Lois Cranston Prize, 2019

"That Night" by Dale Champlin, *The Barbie Diaries* (Just a Lark Books, 2019)

"The Silent Voice" by Jade Rosina McCutcheon, *Small Feather* (Finishing Line Press, 2020)

"Exposed" by Susan Woods Morse, *Hole in the Head Review* (online, Volume 2, Issue 2, May 2021)

"There Will Be Days" by Shawn Aveningo Sanders, *What She Was Wearing* (The Poetry Box, 2019)

The quote by Petrina Coventry is an excerpt from "Why Does Power Abuse Persist?" by Petrina Coventry (https://www.business.com/articles/psychology-of-power-abuse/)

Information for the Gaslighting chapter gleaned from the following websites:

https://www.vox.com/culture/2017/1/21/14315372/what-is-gaslighting-gaslight-movie-ingrid-bergman

https://www.psychologytoday.com/blog/here-there-and-everywhere/201701/11-warning-signs-gaslighting

https://www.psychologytoday.com/blog/toxic-relationships/201801/how-know-if-youre-victim-gaslighting

https://lonerwolf.com/gaslighting/

http://www.dailymail.co.uk/femail/article-5489585/Gaslighting-modern-dating-trend-leave-damaged.html

About the Contributors

Jade Rosina McCutcheon holds a Doctor of Creative Arts and a PhD in feminist film studies. She is a recipient of the Kay Snow Award and received honorary mentions from Kay Snow and the National Federation of Poetry Societies. Jade works with Sable House part-time as an advocate and support facilitator. Her publications include books *Awakening the Performing Body, Embodied Consciousness Performance Technologies*, and *Narrative in Performance*, as well as chapters in edited, peer reviewed journals and books. *Small Feather* (2020) and *The Tossing Dream* (May 2023) were both published by Finishing Line Press. Her poetry has appeared in */pān l dé l mïk/ 2020: An Anthology of Pandemic Poems, Beyond Words*, and in *The Silent World in her Vase*. She is a member of the Mid Valley Poetry Society, The Salem Poetry Project, Artists in Action, and the Oregon Poetry Association. Website: jaderosinamccutcheon.com

Kristin Thomas (K. Thomas) is a native Oregonian whose biggest accomplishment and source of pride is her children and grandchildren. This is her first-time writing poetry, and she finds the lines often compose themselves during her early morning meditation and prayer. She is a survivor of childhood abuse, domestic violence, and sexual violence. Beyond writing, she enjoys being in the forest, near any body of water and laughing.

༄

Diana Blackstone-Helt lives in the Pacific Northwest with her husband and is a recent empty nester after raising two sons. When not writing, she enjoys cooking, hiking, kayaking, and dragon boating.

Candice Campo is an educational psychologist who feels most at home within the Pacific Northwest. She's been involved with the incredible life tool that is poetry since the age of 7 and continues to be a seeker of healthier relationships.

Dale Champlin, the oldest in a family of four sisters, is a feminist poet. She has poems in *The Opiate, Timberline Review, Pif, CatheXis, The Poeming Pigeon*, and many other publications. She is the editor of */pānl dé l mïk/ 2020: An Anthology of Pandemic Poems from the Oregon Poetry Association*. Dale has three poetry collections; *The Barbie Diaries* (Just a Lark Books, 2019), *Callie Comes of Age* (Cirque Press, 2021), and *Isadora* (2022). Three collections, *Leda, Medusa*, and *Andromina, A Stranger in America* are forthcoming. Website: dalechamplin.com

K. Commander is an Oregon poet who is also published in the anthology *Free from Monsters*, (named after her poem), Western Oregon University Press.

Frances Greenwood chooses her information to remain private.

Summer Harlan identifies with and supports healing for all survivors. This is her first-time publishing poetry.

Jarmac is an Oregon based poet and artist who lives to be close to trees. She has doodled most of her life and cares deeply about the abuse of women and children. Honored to contribute to this volume.

Jayme Sue was born and raised in the canyon area of the Willamette Valley, where she still resides. For her, poetry and art are great mediums to communicate intense and complicated emotions and memories, or as a way to start a dialogue to a harder conversation.

Marilyn Johnston began writing poetry as a way to address war and injustices that affect people she holds close and to honor the memories of those she's lost. She is the recipient of an Oregon Literary Arts Fellowship for Writers and winner of the Donna J. Stone National Literary Award for Poetry. Her collection of poems, *Before Igniting*, was published in 2020 (Rippling Brook Press).

Ann L. Lovejoy has lived in various places, including Central America, the East Coast of the U.S, Alaska and currently Salem Oregon. "I contributed to this anthology because I wanted to share my experiences. Life is splendid and wonderful once we escape captivity to achieve self-determination."

Sherri Levine is the author of *Stealing Flowers from the Neighbors* (Kelsay Press, 2021) and *In These Voices* (The Poetry Box, 2019). She was awarded The Lois Cranston Memorial Poetry Prize. She won First Place (Poet's Choice) in the Oregon Poetry Association Spring 2018 biannual poetry contest. Sherri's poetry and other writing have appeared in numerous journals and magazines including *Prairie Schooner, Poet Lore, The Sun Magazine, Jewish Literary Review, and Worcester Review*. Sherri teaches poetry and writing classes in Portland and online. She is the creator and host of Head for the Hills, a monthly poetry series and open mic. Website: Sherrilevine.com

RMae: "In a world drowning in misunderstanding, chaos, confusion, pain and severe disconnection; I paint and write to connect."

L. Medsker: "My early years were marred not by physical trauma but by circumstances around me that I couldn't understand or overcome—and that I couldn't talk about. It felt to me much like what's been confided to me by friends who are sexual abuse survivors, so I share this poem with the hope it will comfort others experiencing that same deep well of pain."

Kelley Morehouse: "I feel that it is very important for me to say what I never had a chance to say. It's hard to put words to the feelings, even to admit the feelings, but it's part of my process in order to break down the denial and accept my story and who I am, as I am."

Susan Woods Morse lives in the Willamette Valley and is an active member of Mid-Valley Poetry Society and a past board member of the Oregon Poetry Association. She is the author of a chapbook, *In the Hush* (Finishing Line Press, 2019) and a full-length collection, *Quilting the Loose Edges* (The Poetry Box, 2023). She contributed to Uprooting because several of her friends are survivors of abuse.

Shannon Rose Riley, MFA, PhD, RSMT/RSME, is an interdisciplinary artist and scholar. She is Professor of Creative Arts and Humanities and Department Chair of Humanities at San José State University. The story in this book is dedicated to her mother, LaVaughn Blanche Riley.

Shawn Aveningo Sanders is the author of *What She Was Wearing*, an inspirational book of poetry & prose which reveals her #metoo secret—from survival to empowerment. Shawn's work has appeared worldwide in over 160 literary journals and anthologies, including *Calyx, Amsterdam Quarterly, American Journal of Poetry, Timberline Review, VoiceCatcher*, and *Poets Reading the News*, to name a few. She's a Pushcart nominee, Best of the Net nominee, co-founder of The Poetry Box press, and managing editor for *The Poeming Pigeon: a journal of poetry & art*. Shawn is a proud mother of three amazing humans and grandmother to one darling baby girl. She shares the creative life with her husband, Robert.

Rebecca Smith is an Oregon artist who has weathered the storm and stands strong with her truth surrounded by the trees of sisterhood.

Cassandra Sumner is an Oregon based writer. "I can now see ahead of me now without a cost. I can feel the new growth emerging from what was nearly lost."

About The Poetry Box®

The Poetry Box, a boutique publishing company in Portland, Oregon, provides a platform for both established and emerging poets to share their words with the world through beautiful printed books and chapbooks.

Feel free to visit the on-line bookstore (thePoetryBox.com), where you'll find more titles including:

Quilting the Loose Edges by Susan Woods Morse

When All Else Fails by Lana Hechtman Ayers

Break-Up Hair & Other Poems by Grace Richards

What She Was Wearing by Shawn Aveningo Sanders

Womanhood & Other Scars by Rebecca Smolen

Listening in the Dark by Suzy Harris

In These Voices by Sherri Levine

Signs by Emily Newberry

Earthwork by Kristin Berger

A Catalog of Small Contentments by Carolyn Martin

Self Dissection by Amelia Diaz Ettinger

This Is the Lightness by Rachel Barton

Tell Her Yes by Ann Farley

Excoriation by Rebecca Smolen

Sophia & Mister Walter Whitman by Penelope Scambly Schott

A Nest in the Heart by Vivienne Popperl

A Starved Heart by Genevieve Lardizabal

Metal Used for Beauty Alone by Claudia Saleeby Savage

and more . . .

Printed in the USA
CPSIA information can be obtained
at www.ICGtesting.com
JSHW071442090923
48059JS00012B/83